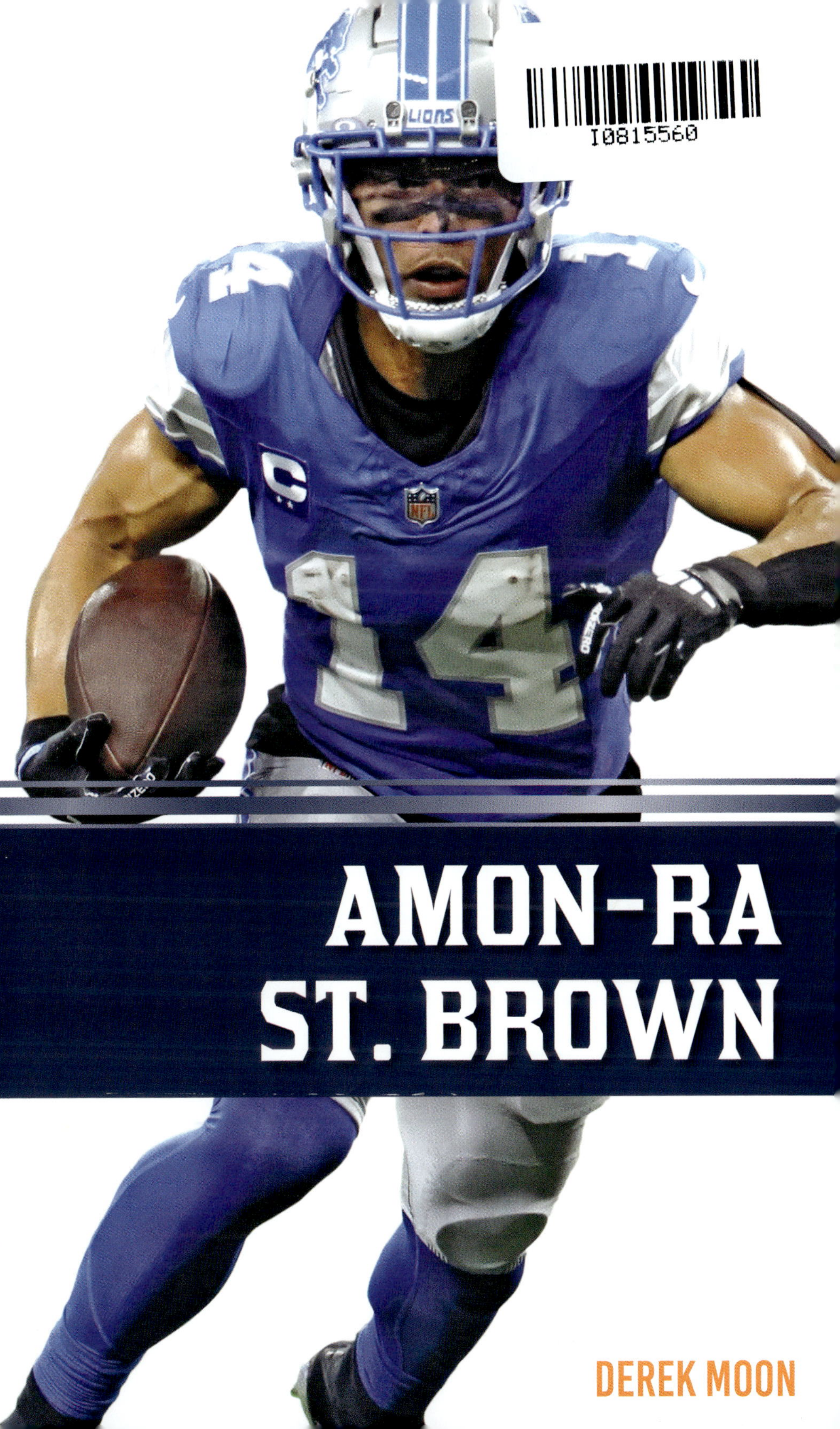

AMON-RA ST. BROWN

DEREK MOON

WWW.APEXEDITIONS.COM

Apex is distributed by North Star Editions:
sales@northstareditions.com | 888-417-0195

Produced for Apex by Red Line Editorial.

Photographs ©: Duane Burleson/AP Images, cover, 1; Rick Osentoski/AP Images, 4–5, 32–33, 37, 40–41; Zachary Silver/AP Images, 6–7, 30–31, 58–59; Federico Gambarini/picture-alliance/dpa/AP Images, 8–9; Shutterstock Images, 10–11, 12–13; Louis Lopez/Cal Sport Media/AP Images, 14–15; David Dennis/Icon Sportswire/AP Images, 16–17; Chris Williams/Icon Sportswire/AP Images, 18–19; Ringo Chiu/AP Images, 20–21; Ric Tapia/AP Images, 22–23; Leon Halip/Getty Images Sport/Getty Images, 24–25; Joe Sargent/Getty Images Sport/Getty Images, 26–27; Ben Liebenberg/AP Images, 28–29; Seth Wenig/AP Images, 34–35; Cooper Neill/AP Images, 38–39; Kyusung Gong/AP Images, 42–43; Ryan Kang/AP Images, 44–45; G. Newman Lowrance/AP Images, 46–47; Paul Sancya/AP Images, 49; David Dermer/AP Images, 50–51; Kevin Sabitus/Getty Images Sport/Getty Images, 52–53, 56–57; Matt Ludtke/AP Images, 54–55

Library of Congress Control Number: 2024951995

ISBN
979-8-89250-726-4 (hardcover)
979-8-89250-778-3 (paperback)
979-8-89250-760-8 (ebook pdf)
979-8-89250-744-8 (hosted ebook)

Printed in the United States of America
Mankato, MN
082025

NOTE TO PARENTS AND EDUCATORS

Apex books are designed to build literacy skills in striving readers. Exciting, high-interest content attracts and holds readers' attention. The text is carefully leveled to allow students to achieve success quickly.

TABLE OF CONTENTS

CHAPTER 1

A WINNING PLAY

Amon-Ra St. Brown took off running. It was fourth down. Only four seconds remained in the game. The Detroit Lions needed a touchdown to win, and they were 11 yards from the end zone. But Minnesota Vikings defenders waited there.

Amon-Ra St. Brown sprints down the field during Week 13 of the 2021 season.

St. Brown reached the goal line. Then he cut to the middle of the field. Two defenders closed in. But they were too late. Quarterback Jared Goff fired a pass. St. Brown hauled it in for a touchdown. The rookie had won the game!

BREAKING THE STREAK

Detroit had already played 11 games in the 2021 season. They lost 10 games. Another game ended in a tie. St. Brown's touchdown snapped the winless streak. In fact, it secured the team's first win in 364 days.

St. Brown finished Week 13 with 10 catches for 86 yards.

CHAPTER 2

WORKING HARD

Amon-Ra St. Brown was born on October 24, 1999. He grew up with two brothers. Amon-Ra's father, John, was a champion bodybuilder. John wanted his sons to be great athletes, too.

Amon-Ra (second from right) is the youngest of the three St. Brown brothers.

Amon-Ra grew up in Anaheim Hills, California. But he also spent lots of time overseas. Amon-Ra's mom, Miriam, was born in Germany. The family spent summers there. So, Amon-Ra learned to speak German at an early age. His mother spoke the language at home. She also made Amon-Ra and his brothers read German books every day.

LEARNING LANGUAGES

Amon-Ra and his brothers also learned to speak French. The boys attended a French elementary school in California. And they spent time at a school in Paris, France.

Anaheim Hills is about 35 miles (56 km) from Los Angeles, California.

Amon-Ra used a passing machine to practice. Starting in middle school, he caught 202 balls a day.

Amon-Ra's parents were strict. Miriam pushed her sons to do well in school. They were expected to get straight A's. John guided the boys in sports. He taught them to work hard. They lifted weights. They ate lots of food to help build muscle. All three boys became great athletes. And no one worked harder than Amon-Ra.

NOTICEABLE NAMES

John Brown felt that his name was too boring. He wanted his kids' names to be memorable. Equanimeous was named after a character in a book. Osiris and Amon-Ra were named after Egyptian gods. John also added *St.* to their last name.

Amon-Ra went to Mater Dei High School. The school is known for its successful football program. Amon-Ra thrived. Experts said he was one of the best high school players in the country. Every college team wanted him. Amon-Ra picked the University of Southern California (USC).

THE RIGHT FIT

Amon-Ra grew up an hour from USC. The school is known for developing wide receivers. NFL standout Nelson Agholor went there. So did JuJu Smith-Schuster.

Amon-Ra scores a touchdown during a 2017 state title game.

CHAPTER 3

COLLEGE STAR

Amon-Ra St. Brown joined quarterback JT Daniels at USC. The two had been high school teammates. St. Brown had a great first game. In the fourth quarter, he raced down the field. Daniels lofted a pass. They connected for a 43-yard touchdown.

St. Brown had 7 catches for 98 yards in his first college game.

St. Brown could change direction quickly. Defenders had trouble sticking with him.

Often, college freshmen don't play much. But St. Brown was ready. He could make plays all over the field. No USC player caught more passes in 2018.

St. Brown was even better in his second year. He caught 77 passes for 1,042 yards. He added more yards as a runner and punt returner.

FOOTBALL FAMILY

All three St. Brown brothers played wide receiver in college. Equanimeous starred at Notre Dame. Osiris played at Stanford.

COVID-19 shut down much of the world in 2020. USC played just six games. Usually, the schedule is twice as long. St. Brown made the most of the short season. He scored seven touchdowns. USC finished the year with a 5–1 record.

FOUR FOR FOUR

Nobody could stop St. Brown on December 6, 2020. He caught four passes in the first quarter. All four went for touchdowns. USC easily beat Washington State 38–13.

St. Brown makes a difficult touchdown catch against Washington State.

St. Brown runs the 40-yard dash for NFL scouts.

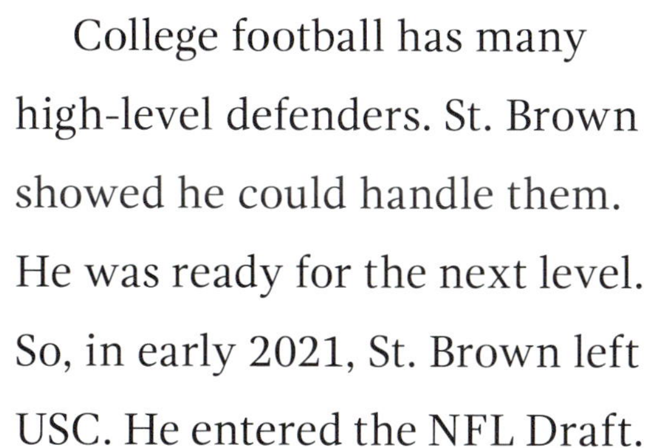

College football has many high-level defenders. St. Brown showed he could handle them. He was ready for the next level. So, in early 2021, St. Brown left USC. He entered the NFL Draft.

SMART BUT SMALL

Scouts praised St. Brown's skills. They also called him a smart player. But they worried about his smaller size. He also wasn't as fast as other receivers.

Some people thought St. Brown could be picked in the first round of the NFL Draft. However, things didn't go as St. Brown hoped. No team selected him in the first round. Then the second round passed. So did the third round. Finally, the Detroit Lions selected St. Brown in the fourth round. He had fallen to the 112th pick.

NOTEBOOK OF NAMES

St. Brown keeps a notebook. One page has a list of 16 names. They are the receivers taken before him in the 2021 draft. St. Brown often reads the list for motivation. He wants to prove he's better than the other receivers.

St. Brown practiced hard and learned plays quickly. That impressed the Lions' coaches.

CHAPTER 4

WELCOME TO THE NFL

The Lions had struggled in 2020. Then, in 2021, St. Brown's rookie season started out even worse. Detroit went winless in its first 11 games. St. Brown didn't play much. But he showed promise.

St. Brown makes a catch during a 2021 preseason game.

Detroit's coaches started using St. Brown in new ways. The wide receiver moved around more before the snap. He ran different kinds of routes. Sometimes St. Brown even ran the ball. Defenses didn't know what to expect. The approach worked. St. Brown started making more catches. The Lions' offense improved.

PRACTICE MAKES PERFECT

St. Brown trained hard throughout the season. In the weight room, he lifted heavier weights than other receivers. After practice, he stayed on the field to do extra catching and sprinting drills.

St. Brown used eye and body movements to fake out defenders. They didn't know where he would run.

Soon, St. Brown's hard work paid off. The Lions kept throwing to him. And he rarely dropped passes. The team went 3–3 in its last 6 games. St. Brown had 51 catches in those games. That brought him to 90 catches for the season. No Lions receiver had more. St. Brown also led the team in receiving yards.

MR. DECEMBER

In December 2021, St. Brown had 35 catches for 340 yards. He also had three touchdowns. The NFL named St. Brown the Offensive Rookie of the Month.

St. Brown dropped only one pass in the 2021 season.

St. Brown had 11 catches for 114 yards in Week 13 of the 2022 season.

The Lions' first game of the 2022 regular season was against the Philadelphia Eagles. St. Brown caught a touchdown pass. But Detroit still lost. The next few weeks weren't much better. The Lions lost six of their first seven games. St. Brown also injured his ankle. He missed a game. It was a disappointing start.

St. Brown was the youngest player in Lions history to have 1,000 receiving yards in a season.

Suddenly, the Lions started winning. St. Brown was a big reason for their success. Quarterback Jared Goff liked passing to him. St. Brown often found holes in the defense. In one win, he caught 10 passes. In another win, he caught 11. Detroit won 8 of its final 10 games. After the season, St. Brown took part in his first Pro Bowl Games.

TOP 100

Each year, NFL players rank one another. St. Brown's 2022 season earned the league's attention. The players voted him as one of the NFL's 100 best players.

IN THE SPOTLIGHT

RECEIVING RECORDS

The Lions hosted the Washington Commanders on September 18, 2022. St. Brown's second catch of the game went for 49 yards. He caught a touchdown pass soon after. It was his sixth game in a row with a touchdown. That tied a team record. But he wasn't done yet.

St. Brown added a second touchdown in the fourth quarter. He ended the game with nine catches. It was his eighth straight game with at least eight catches. That tied an NFL record.

ST. BROWN HAD 116 RECEIVING YARDS AND 68 RUSHING YARDS AGAINST THE WASHINGTON COMMANDERS.

LIONS
14
adidas

CHAPTER 5

KING OF THE LIONS

The Lions opened the 2023 season in Kansas City. It was a huge test. The Chiefs were Super Bowl champs. St. Brown was ready. He scored a 9-yard touchdown to put Detroit up 7–0. The Lions went on to win by one point.

Before 2023, Detroit had lost or tied in five straight season openers.

All year, other teams knew the ball was going to St. Brown. But they still couldn't stop him. He broke tackles. He made diving catches. And the Lions kept winning. In Week 10, St. Brown caught eight passes. They went for 156 yards. It was his best performance yet.

TOUGH PLAYER

St. Brown injured his toe in Week 2 of the 2023 season. The next week, he hurt a muscle. Later in the season, he got sick. Despite these setbacks, St. Brown missed only one game.

St. Brown wasn't just good at catching. He was also a strong blocker.

St. Brown helped turn the Lions into winners. He had another big game to end the 2023 regular season. The Lions won, giving them a record of 12–5. They hadn't won 12 games since 1991. The wins gave Detroit a division title. It was the team's first title in 30 years.

TOP TALENT

St. Brown racked up 1,515 receiving yards in 2023. That was third most in the league. He also caught 10 touchdown passes. Only three players had more. St. Brown had shown that he was a top receiver.

St. Brown snagged 119 catches in 2023.

St. Brown celebrates during a playoff game against the Los Angeles Rams.

Detroit faced the Los Angeles Rams in the playoffs. Lions fans badly wanted a win. But the Rams kept it close. Detroit clung to a one-point lead. Then Jared Goff threw to St. Brown. The 11-yard catch was good for a first down. After that, Detroit let time run out. It was the Lions' first playoff win in 32 years.

THE RETURN

The Lions' first playoff game after the 2023 regular season included some extra drama. Matthew Stafford had spent 12 years with the Lions. But his teams didn't have much success. Stafford was traded to the Rams in 2021. Now, the Lions faced their former quarterback.

In the second round of the playoffs, St. Brown had 8 catches for 77 yards.

The next week, Detroit faced the Tampa Bay Buccaneers. St. Brown scored a touchdown. It sealed another playoff win. One more win would send the Lions to the Super Bowl.

The conference title game started well. St. Brown made some big catches. Detroit led 24–7 at halftime. But the San Francisco 49ers rallied to win. Detroit's dream season was over.

IN THE SPOTLIGHT

CAN'T CATCH HIM

Detroit played the Minnesota Vikings in the last game of the 2023 regular season. In the fourth quarter, Jared Goff dropped back to pass. St. Brown raced up the left sideline.

St. Brown caught a long pass at Minnesota's 40-yard line. Then he sprinted back toward the middle of the field. Minnesota finally cornered him around the 15-yard line. So, St. Brown cut back. A defender grabbed him. But there was no stopping the receiver. St. Brown's 70-yard touchdown put Detroit up 27–13. The catch helped Detroit win the game.

ST. BROWN HAD 144 YARDS AGAINST THE VIKINGS.

VIKINGS

CHAPTER 6

SUPERSTAR

St. Brown had always been driven. He tried to work harder than anyone else. By his third season, St. Brown was one of the NFL's best players. He was named an All-Pro.

Detroit's 2024 opener was a rematch of the playoffs. The Lions beat the Rams 26–20.

The Lions knew they had a special talent. In 2024, they offered St. Brown a new deal. He agreed to stay in Detroit four more years. In return, the Lions would pay him at least $77 million. That was the biggest deal ever for a wide receiver.

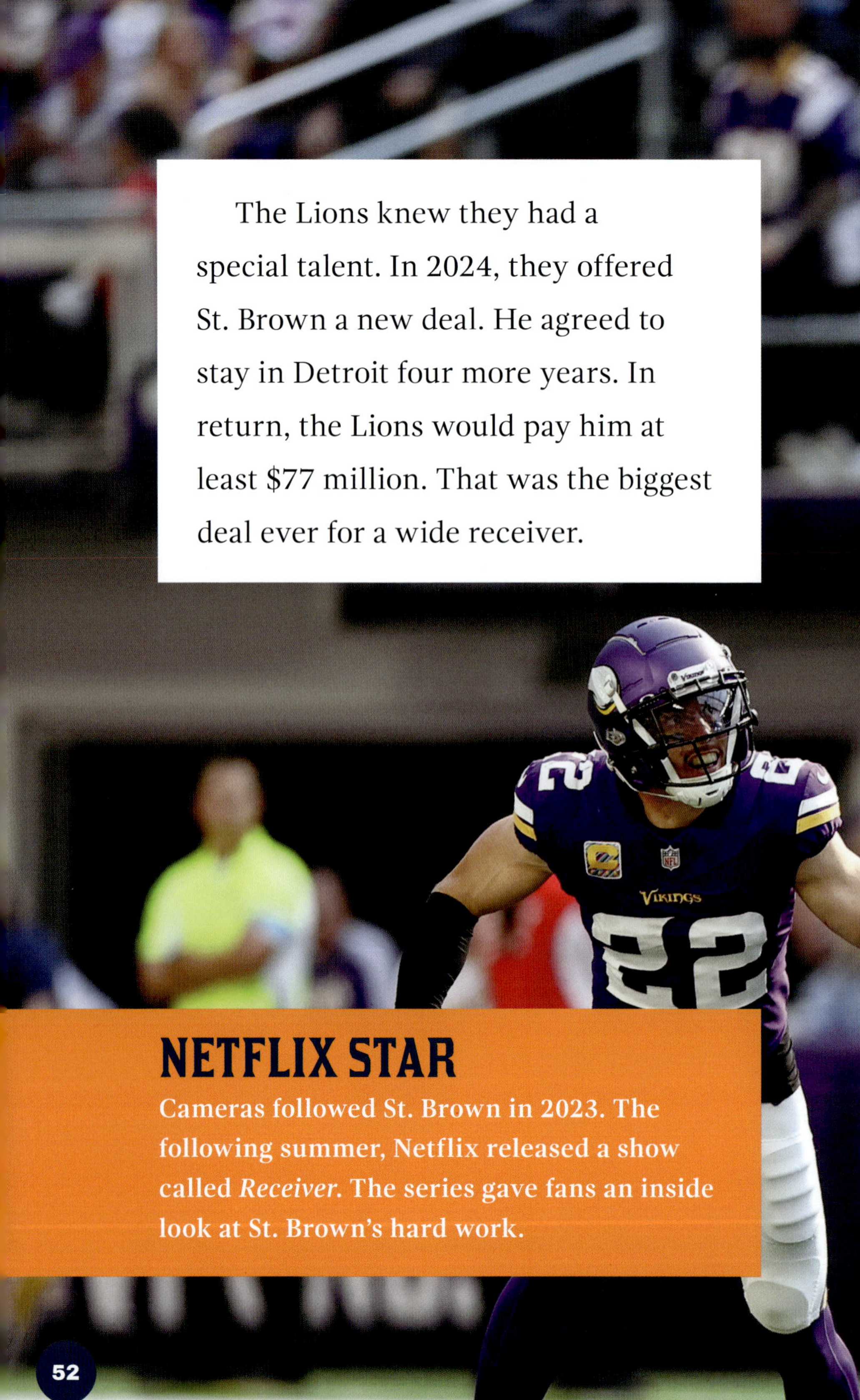

NETFLIX STAR

Cameras followed St. Brown in 2023. The following summer, Netflix released a show called *Receiver.* The series gave fans an inside look at St. Brown's hard work.

In 2024, St. Brown had 112 receiving yards and a touchdown in a Week 7 win.

St. Brown had a toe-tapping touchdown catch in a Week 14 game against the Green Bay Packers.

Detroit had high expectations in 2024. Many of the team's best players returned. The Lions won 12 of their first 13 games. In three of those games, St. Brown racked up more than 100 receiving yards. However, several key players got injured during the season.

GREAT GAME

One of St. Brown's best games of 2024 came in Week 11. He caught every pass thrown his way. Two of those catches went for touchdowns. St. Brown finished the game with 161 receiving yards.

In Week 18, Detroit faced the Minnesota Vikings. The winner of the game would earn a first-round bye in the playoffs. St. Brown had 77 receiving yards. He helped Detroit crush Minnesota 31–9. For the first time in team history, the Lions had the top seed in the playoffs. However, Detroit's injury troubles were too much to overcome. The Lions lost in the second round. St. Brown's Super Bowl dreams would have to wait.

St. Brown finished the 2024 regular season with 1,263 yards and 12 touchdowns.

TIMELINE

1999

Amon-Ra St. Brown is born on October 24 in Anaheim Hills, California.

2018

St. Brown catches a 43-yard pass in his first game with USC.

2020

St. Brown scores touchdowns on his first four catches in a win over Washington State.

2021

On May 1, the Detroit Lions select St. Brown with the 112th pick in the NFL Draft.

2021

On December 5, St. Brown's last-second touchdown gives the Lions their first win in nearly a year.

2023
On February 5, St. Brown takes part in his first Pro Bowl Games.

2023
On November 12, St. Brown records a career-high 156 receiving yards against the Los Angeles Chargers.

2024
On January 21, St. Brown scores a touchdown as the Lions win their second playoff game in a row.

2024
On April 24, St. Brown agrees to a new deal with Detroit, making him the highest-paid receiver ever.

2025
On January 5, St. Brown helps the Lions clinch a No. 1 playoff seed for the first time in team history.

COMPREHENSION QUESTIONS

Write your answers on a separate piece of paper.

1. Write a paragraph that explains the main ideas of Chapter 2.
2. What do you think made Amon-Ra St. Brown ready to succeed as a college football player?
3. After the 2023 season, what team did the Lions play in the conference title game?

    A. Los Angeles Chargers
    B. Minnesota Vikings
    C. San Francisco 49ers

4. How many seasons did Amon-Ra St. Brown play at USC?

    A. two
    B. three
    C. four

5. What does **thrived** mean in this book?

Amon-Ra ***thrived****. Experts said he was one of the best high school players in the country.*

A. did poorly
B. did well
C. did not play

6. What does **disappointing** mean in this book?

The Lions lost six of their first seven games. St. Brown also injured his ankle. He missed a game. It was a ***disappointing*** *start.*

A. better than what happened before
B. not having any problems or challenges
C. not what was wanted or hoped for

Answer key on page 64.

GLOSSARY

bodybuilder
A person who works to build big muscles.

conference
A group of teams that make up part of a sports league.

developing
Helping people become better players.

division
In the NFL, a group of teams that make up part of a conference.

draft
A system that lets teams select new players coming into the league.

freshmen
Students in their first year of college.

motivation
Reasons for working hard.

playoffs
A set of games played after the regular season to decide which team is the champion.

rookie
An athlete in his or her first year as a professional player.

scouts
People who travel around to look for new, talented players.

TO LEARN MORE

BOOKS

Adamson, Thomas K. *The Detroit Lions.* Bellwether Media, 2024.

Anderson, Josh. *G.O.A.T. Football Wide Receivers.* Lerner Publications, 2024.

Coleman, Ted. *Detroit Lions All-Time Greats.* Press Box Books, 2022.

ONLINE RESOURCES

Visit **www.apexeditions.com** to find links and resources related to this title.

ABOUT THE AUTHOR

Derek Moon is an author and avid Stratego player who lives in Watertown, Massachusetts, with his wife and daughter.

INDEX

ANSWER KEY:

1. Answers will vary; 2. Answers will vary; 3. C; 4. B; 5. B; 6. C